MW01250620

Gravity

By Myrl Shireman
Illustrated By John E. Kaufmann

COPYRIGHT © 2006 Mark Twain Media, Inc.

ISBN 1-58037-362-3

Printing No. D04116

Mark Twain Media, Inc., Publishers
Distributed by Carson-Dellosa Publishing Company, Inc.

Level 4: Book 2

Gravity

Have you ever thrown a ball to someone? Did you wonder why the ball fell back to Earth? Why didn't the ball fly off into space? When you throw the ball, it climbs higher as it leaves your hand. After leaving your hand, the ball is at its greatest speed. As the ball climbs higher, it begins to slow down. Then it begins to fall back to Earth. The shape of the path of the ball as it climbs higher and falls back to Earth has a name. The path is called a **parabola**.

Earth's gravity pulls the ball back to Earth.

When the ball leaves your hand, it is trying to break free from the earth's gravity. The ball is trying to fly into space. However, the earth is pulling on the ball, trying to pull it back to Earth. **Gravity** is a force that attracts one object to another. When you throw a ball into the air, it is trying to break free from the earth. The earth is trying to pull the ball back. Earth wins when the ball begins to fall back to Earth.

3

Slowly, the ball begins to fall back to Earth. As the ball falls, its speed begins to increase. When the ball hits the glove of your friend, you hear a loud smack. The loud smack is because the ball was gaining speed as it fell. Sometimes, the speed is great enough to cause the ball to sting when it is caught. The shape of the path of the ball as it climbed higher and then fell back to Earth was a parabola.

parabola

The force of gravity

But what if you were on the moon playing catch with your friend? When you throw the ball, would it go farther on the moon than on Earth? Would you weigh more or less on the moon? Is gravity greater on the moon than on Earth? Space travel helped answer these questions. The first man on the moon took a giant leap. He found he could leap much farther on the moon than he could on Earth. What does that tell you about gravity on the moon?

Weight

On Earth or on the moon, you do not notice the pull of gravity. But when you step on a scale, the scale shows your **weight**. The scale tells you that gravity is pulling on you. It is pulling you toward the center of the earth. It is the force of gravity that causes your weight to show on the scale.

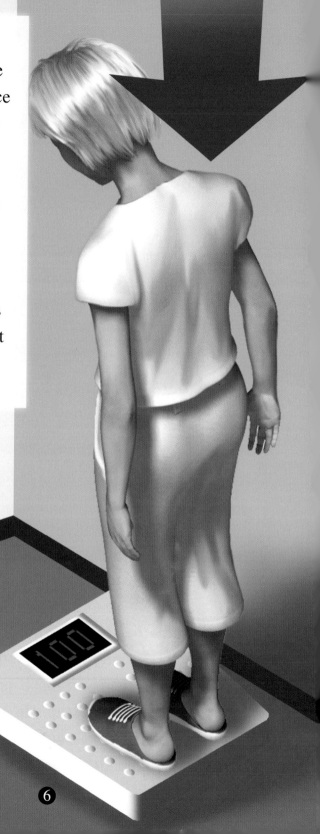

If you weigh 20 pounds on the moon, you weigh much more on Earth. On Earth, you would weigh 120 pounds. You would weigh six times more on Earth than on the moon, because the pull of gravity is much greater on Earth. Because the pull of gravity is less on the moon, you could throw the ball farther on the moon. You could also hit the ball and jump much farther.

Space

Why do the planets stay in orbit around the sun? Why does the moon stay in orbit around the earth? Gravity keeps them in orbit. It also makes fruit fall down from a tree. All things on Earth fall to Earth because of gravity. Gravity is the force that makes objects attract each other. The closer objects are, the greater the force. When objects are far apart, the force is less. Therefore, the earth does not attract objects as much as they get farther from the earth's gravity. As an object gets farther from the earth, it weighs less. Finally, it breaks free from the earth's gravity. The object can speed off into space.

When a spaceship is **launched**, or shot into space, the earth and spaceship attract each other. The spaceship is trying to break free from Earth. Earth is trying to pull it back. The farther the spaceship gets from Earth, the less the pull of gravity. Finally, the spaceship breaks free from Earth's gravity. The earth's gravity can no longer pull the spaceship back. Inside the rocket, objects now float in the air. If a person in the spaceship steps on a scale, his or her weight is zero.

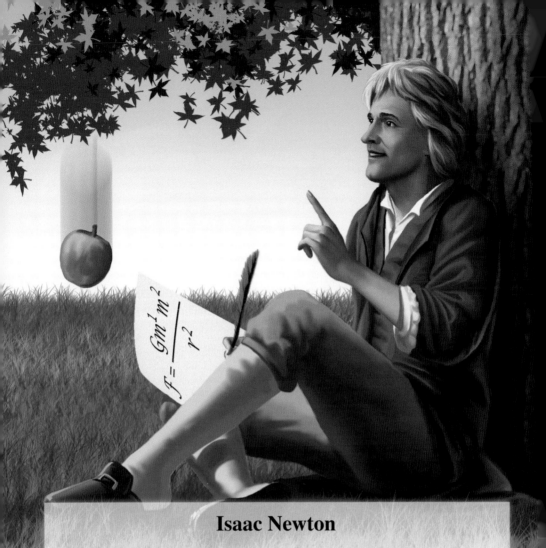

$$F = \frac{Gm^1m^2}{r^2}$$

Isaac Newton

Isaac Newton was a scientist who lived many years ago. He was always thinking about why things happen. One story tells how one day he was sitting in his garden. While there, he saw an apple fall from a tree. He wondered, "Why did the apple fall down? Why didn't it fall up?" He thought that it was because of some **force**, a power or energy. It took Newton many years before he could explain the force. He was very good in math. After many years, he used math to show how the force works. Later, you will use Newton's math in your science classes.

After thinking some more, Newton called the force gravity. He said that the earth attracts objects to its center. When the apple fell, it was falling toward the center of the earth. He said that the earth and the apple attract each other. All objects attract each other. People in the same room attract each other. However, the force is very small— so small that it is not noticed.

Gravity

Mass

Why did the apple fall to Earth? The earth is larger than the apple. It has more **mass**. The more mass, the greater the force of gravity. To understand mass, think of two balls. They are the same size. However, one is made of iron. The other is a hollow plastic ball. The iron ball weighs more. It has more mass.

20

1

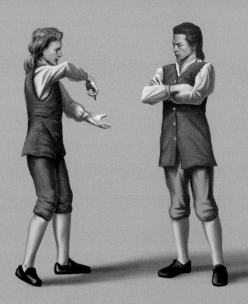

Newton started telling other people about gravity. He said that every object attracts other objects. Newton said every object on Earth was pulled toward the center of the earth. Many people did not believe Newton. They could not feel the pull of the force he was talking about. Newton said this force could not be seen. It was many years before many people thought Newton was right. Newton said that two objects attract each other in a special way. The closer the objects are, the more they attract. The farther apart they are, the less they attract.

Objects that are close together attract each other more than objects that are farther apart.

1sec.

2sec.

3sec.

4sec.

5sec.

6sec.

When an object falls, it gains speed. Each second it falls faster. Therefore, each second an object falls farther. Because of gravity, objects gain speed as they fall. An apple hanging on a tree has a speed of zero. When it begins to fall, each second it falls farther. The apple gains speed. The apple doesn't fall far before it hits the ground. What happens when an object is dropped from a tall building? Each second an object falls, its speed is about 22 miles per hour (mph) greater.

Think about this. Two balls of the same size are dropped from a tall building. One ball is iron. It has more mass than the other ball. It weighs more. Will the heavy ball fall faster than the lighter one? Will the heavy ball and lighter ball fall at the same speed? Will an apple fall faster than a feather? For many years, people thought that heavier objects fell faster. The apple fell quickly to the ground, while the feather floated.

However, scientists thought that the apple and the feather fell at the same speed. They thought that without the resistance from the air, the apple and feather would reach the ground at the same time. To prove this, objects were dropped in a vacuum. In the **vacuum**, there was no air to resist the fall. Without air, the objects fell at the same speed.

In the open air, a heavy ball made of iron will hit the ground before a light ball made of foam.

Balls dropped in a vacuum tube both hit the ground at the same time.

15

Orbits

The earth has more mass than the moon. You may be wondering why the moon doesn't fall into the earth. The moon is in **orbit** around the earth. In its orbit, it is always falling toward the earth. But the moon travels very fast in its orbit. The earth's surface is curved. While the moon is falling, the earth's surface curves away from the moon. As the moon orbits the earth, it is falling toward the earth, but it falls around the curved surface of the earth. It never falls to Earth. A spacecraft does the same thing as it orbits the earth.

You also may be wondering why the planets stay in orbit around the sun. Gravity holds all of the planets in orbit around the sun. Why does the moon orbit the earth? Gravity holds the moon in orbit around the earth. The moons around other planets are also held in orbit by gravity.